The Spice Whisperer

BIBI KASRAI

The Spice Whisperer
By Bibi Kasrai

4

Editor: Shideh Etaat
Photographer: Sanam Salehian
Makeup Artist: Jenn Badel
Graphic Design: Farshid Saffari

ISBN
978-1-59584-399-9

Ketab Corp.
1419 Westwood Blvd.
Los Angeles CA 90024 USA
Tel.: 310-477-7477
Fax: 310-444-7176
www.ketab.com

Library of Congress Cataloging-in-Publishing Data
Cooking - Persian cooking - International Cooking - Memoirs

To my beloved Kasra and Ava. I hope one day
you will understand that everything I've done has
been for the two of you.
To my mom who is and has always been my rock.
To my brother and sister who are my wings.
To my inspiration and my angel, Mamaee, who is
cooking in heaven now.
To my dad whose every drop of passionate blood
runs through my veins.
And yes, even to you!

Acknowledgements

6

First and foremost I have to thank the characters on these pages because this isn't a work of fiction and without them there would be no book. Many of them are absent, and I've saved their stories for the next book.

My gratitude to Shideh Etaat, my young editor. It was a long and tortuous process to finally find her, with many guiding angels in between. She shaped the book into this readable version you are holding in your hands. Special thanks to my dear Sanam Salehian for patiently and quietly coming in and out of Harvard Cookin' Girl and taking photographs.

Special thanks to my publisher- Mr. Bijan Khalili of Sherkat-e Ketab for having faith in me as a novice writer and for supporting Iranian diaspora writers for 33 years and of course the book designer Farshid Saffari.

Thanks to all my colleagues at Harvard Cookin' Girl whom I love dearly, for giving me enough breathing room to accomplish this project on top of my daily job. And finally thanks to all the bad bosses who made me turn my back to corporate America and follow my dream one plate at a time.

Bibi Kasrai

CONTENTS

Introduction ....

Grandmother Knows Best ....

Grandmother's Plum Chicken Makes All Bad Things Go Away (Khoresh Aloo) ....

Crush In The Time Of Cholera (Adas Polo) ....

Sergei, the Drunk Soldier (Borchst) ....

Fighting or Feasting (Chicken Tagine with Mejool Dates) ....

Food That Lifts You Up (Chana Bateta) ....

New Year's Eve In A Crowded Moscow Dorm (Gheimeh Bademjan) ....

How To Eat Like Royalty (Bahn Mi) ....

Mourning For Love The Western Way (Makowiec) ....

Love And Sushi (Bibi's California Sushi) ....

You Are Worthy (Far Breton) ....

Something Out of Nothing (Pineapple Flambé) ....

The Replicator (Pad Thai) ....

The Rice Rules (Persian Jasmine Rice) ....

The Half Human (Pasta Spontanea) ....

Love At First Taste (Shevid Polo Gooshte Loobia) ....

Introduction Excerpt

My parents never let me into the kitchen. I was a smart girl, learned languages easily, did well in school, and they believed that a kitchen was no place for a girl like me. It was my grandmother who allowed me to enter this magical world of food as a young girl, although I mostly watched and didn't ask too many questions. It was the old, brick house she had built with my grandfather on "Spring" Street in Tehran that became my refuge.

Many years later, it would become difficult to find any kind of refuge though as the Islamic Revolution ignited through our country. My family had helped the Jews, the Bahai's and royalist friends escape, but now it was our turn. My mother came up with a plan to hire smugglers that would hopefully take us to France where all our European dreams would come true; except we ended up in Moscow via Afghanistan.

On a frigid Moscow day, I walked into the communal kitchen at the end of my dormitory's hallway. It was a tightly squeezed space, and was buzzing with people of all colors, an array of exotic languages, and most importantly the scent of each country coming to life through the delectable meals that people cooked in this kitchen. I immediately noticed three women – one standing, glaring at her pan and stirring something, another wearing a head scarf, chopping parsley, garlic and tomatoes, her spices neatly stacked next to her, and the third making something that looked and smelled very familiar to me. I had watched my grandmother cook hundreds of dishes, and although she would offer me a taste through the cooking process, she never formally taught me which ingredients were which and how much of each I needed to use. She showed me how to love and appreciate food, not necessarily how to cook it, so not knowing my way around the kitchen I quietly observed the three women. At eighteen years old I thought I knew everything. Even though my country was in shambles, I still believed that Iran had the most beautiful sky, the most prophetic poetry, and the most delicious food. But as I inhaled all these different aromas mixing in the air, I found myself hungry for dishes from other places, ingredients I'd never tasted before.

11

I shyly asked the woman close to me where she was from. Her Russian was worse than mine, something I hardly thought possible, but I understood that she was from Lebanon and so I spoke French to her and she explained to me that she was making tabouleh. As she described tabouleh to me I quickly realized how similar it is to the Persian Shiraz salad. She offered me a taste, but looking at her headscarf I felt that whatever she'd made, it couldn't be that good. It wasn't her cooking I didn't trust, but more how that scarf represented the very regime that had brought me to Moscow.

The second woman was making a pudding with rice flour and rosewater. I moved closer to her, remembering the smell of days of mourning when my grandmother made her special rosewater pudding and gave it as an offering to the poor. I smiled at the woman and she told me that she was from Israel. I dismissed her too. She was beautiful, too beautiful even, but when I looked at her I saw the misfortunes of all the Palestinians I'd watched on television. Despite all of this I found myself wanting a spoonful of the goodness she was making.

I turned toward the third woman and the familiar smell of basmati rice and learned that the delicate woman was a new Afghan bride. Once again, my ego took over and I believed that there was no way the rice she was making could be as good as the rice people made in my country. Still, hunger gnawed at my stomach, and I engaged in conversation with the trio. As they asked me questions and I slowly revealed my lack of kitchen savvy the tables suddenly turned. The women confided that they felt sorry for me because they learned that I couldn't even make tea if my life depended on it, which sent all of us into a laughing fit. Each woman generously offered me the first real, homemade food I'd had in months. I was ashamed – I walked in seeing them as representatives of their respective governments and they were beautiful, skillful, and lovely women who without even a question shared their food with me.

Despite the often brutal realities of our world, we choose how we see things, and from that day on I chose to see our connected humanity through food. No matter what your skin color, or what god you pray to, or what land you fled from, you still enjoy sitting around a table and taking in the ingredients and flavors that have been passed down to you. Behind every recipe is a story, and behind every story is someone who finds solace and joy in the ritual of cooking, and of course eating too.

Harvard Cookin' School has been a long time in the making. If someone had told me while at Harvard Business School that this would be my destiny, I would've laughed at them. I worked for big corporations for many years, helped develop non-profit organizations, but one day I really looked at my life. I had many accomplishments, but nothing of great meaning to me. I decided to quit my job and start cooking with my kids. I wanted them to know their way around a kitchen, and I even involved their friends during play dates. I soon had phone calls from mothers raving about how their sons and daughters were learning about math through our cooking lessons and were more curious about the food they were eating. I don't believe in radicalism when it comes to eating. I tell my students all the time to eat! Eat well, and eat everything! But do it in a way that makes it a positive and exciting aspect of your everyday life. It's possible to be healthy and eat really good food too, I promise.

It was difficult finding a name for this book. I loved cooking for my friends long before it was considered to be hip, and one day one of my good friends Gordafarid, a very well-known Iranian naghalor storyteller, watched me prepare a meal before a dinner party I was hosting. After the guests arrived, we caught up with one another, and finally ate our dinner. People started complimenting me on my cooking and Gordafarid exclaimed to all that I was in fact an advieh baz. Advieh means spice in Farsi, but more like the magical blend of a few spices that turn an ordinary dish into an extraordinary culinary delight. Every cook takes pride in obtaining the perfect mixture, and it's the unattainable fairy dust of Eastern cooking. She claimed that the way my hands moved while I cooked, it was as if I was doing a dance with the spices, actually having a conversation with them.

I never saw my grandmother after I left Iran, and I would like to dedicate this book to the woman who was my first teacher and inspiration, the woman who made jams out of rose petals and watermelon rinds, and who would take in the sick and bring them back to health, the woman who taught me how to bring food to the table with the most important ingredient of all- love.

My grandmother was a mix between Martha Stewart and Mother Teresa. She was a plump woman who always wore loose fitting clothes, and despite her round body had small, kind hands. She didn't just walk into a room, she waddled in, always with a smile , ready to cook or sew or help someone learn a new skill that would better their life. We called her Mamaee and her house was the most comforting place on earth, and this sense of peace was baked into the food that emerged from her kitchen.

Mamaee had rituals that would never go dismissed or forgotten no matter how the day went. There could be a blizzard outside or it could be so humid and hot that the thought of staying inside was unbearable, but she stuck to them as if they were her promise to God. Breakfast was crucial as was the early afternoon nap, but one of my favorites was the late afternoon tea and snack that always came after watering the garden, of course. First, she had to water the garden exactly when the sun started its descent and the smell of fresh earth mingled with jasmine; lilies and mint in the garden took over the air. Next, she would cut a few sprigs of cilantro, mint, and chives, and pull a handful of radishes, fresh from the ground to be carefully washed and dried. Mamaee would then turn to the preparation of the tea which she made in an old brass Russian Samovar and was left to seep for exactly 20 minutes while warming the bread that

she'd purchased fresh that morning from the neighborhood baker who baked the Barbari, Sangak, or Lavash bread in an underground oven. There would always be a long line, and it was a common sight to have people approaching Mamaee in line for life advice or inquiring if she knew any suitors for their daughter. I was especially excited for this snack on days she asked for extra sesame seeds on the bread.

She neatly stacked the bread, the fresh Feta and Persian cucumbers from the neighborhood grocer, a bowl of golden raisins, and her homegrown herbs and radishes on the platter. Tea was served in the garden in the gathering dusk, in small, ornate, crystal cups rimmed with gold. Next to each cup of tea she would put a few saffron and rosewater sugar cubes that could be placed in our mouths to melt as we took sips of the tea, or to be added directly to the tea to sweeten each sip. She would give my cousins and siblings a small, silver platter to place our plates, teacups, bread and other goodies. Next, she laid a few jasmine blossoms she'd cut from the garden, their gentle, sweet scent mixing with the spicier, sharper herbs. She believed that food should be enjoyed by all the senses, and that if we didn't want to make the eyes or ears jealous, we had to make an offering to them too. She opened the waterspout in the middle of the garden fountain so our ears might enjoy the sound of water.

Mamaee would help us put the Feta at the center of the bread, and then she would layer in a few leaves of mint, chive, and tarragon, the chopped radish or cucumber, and a sprinkle of golden raisins, then roll it tightly and hand it to us. Sometimes we would dunk the roll in sweet tea the way the French do with their coffee and croissants. As we quietly snacked and sipped, she would then begin telling us stories about her childhood. When I was a little girl I would have given anything to have one of those afternoon snacks. It was more than just the comforting food we ate, it was the peaceful and all-knowing way my grandmother sat there, the way the birds chirped around her as if they were her friends, the wisdom she shared with us while my mouth was full and my eyes waited patiently for the moon.

Grandmother's Plum Chicken Makes All Bad Things Go Away
Khoresh Aloo

20

I've never found a recipe for Plum Chicken in Persian recipe books, but some of my fondest childhood memories are of this meal, which my grandmother cooked expertly. When things just weren't going my way, when I would get into arguments with my mother or siblings, I loved to escape to Mamaee's house. It was our ritual that on days when I wasn't feeling so happy, she would offer to make Plum Chicken. As the sights and scents of sour and sweet permeated the entire kitchen, all of my worries would evaporate.

For many years, almost three decades, I had no idea why it was that when my family sat down to eat this delightful dish we'd start telling wonderful stories, laughing until we cried,

shedding tears of joy, and then a calming unity would consume us.

"If you eat too much saffron you're going to die," Mamaee would warn us.

"We're going to die laughing?" I would ask, spreading my contagious laughter to my aunts and cousins, to Mamaee who soon had tears rolling down her face.

There was nothing more beautiful than laughing about absolutely nothing at all. Mamaee had many secrets, an old world wisdom really– the kind that was intuitively authentic and simple in its practicality. When it came to Plum Chicken, she knew all too well that if you consume a generous amount of saffron, you'd find yourself laughing more than you thought possible as saffron is the world's most expensive natural Prozac. I recreated the Plum Chicken of my child-

hood here to celebrate Mamaee's memory and to continue her tradition of bringing happiness to the table.

With only memories of her, I had to rely on my taste buds, intuition, and a large dose of trial and error in order to recreate her Plum Chicken just as I remember it – soft plums that melt instantaneously as they come into contact with your taste buds, releasing a tangy and sweet burst of flavor that complements the savory tomato paste and tender chicken. The genius of this dish is that like vintage wine, it only improves with time so you can make the braise the day before. After the dish cools it should be refrigerated. Then, remove the dish an hour before you are ready to serve and let it come to room temperature. Heat over a low flame until warmed through and serve with Bibi's Persian Saffron Rice.

Grandmother's Plum Chicken

INGREDIENTS:

- **2-3 tbsp of olive or vegetable oil**
- **1 onion - diced**
- **1 clove of garlic - minced**
- **6-8 chicken tenders - cubed**
- **1 or 2 tbsp of tomato paste (to taste)**
- **½ tsp cumin**
- **Salt and pepper to taste**
- **1-2 tsp saffron (depending on how much you are willing to invest in this dish!)**
- **1 sugar cube**
- **2 tbsp of hot water**
- **1 to 2 cups of chicken broth**
- **Dried Bokhara plums or Golden Plums (soaked for 30-60 min in a cup of hot water)**

PREPARATION:

Heat the olive oil over medium high heat; add the onions and sauté, stirring occasionally until golden. Add the garlic and let onions and garlic lightly caramelize to golden brown. Add the chicken and cook on each side, turning once, until lightly browned. Add the plums with the water and tomato paste. Crush saffron with one sugar cube in a mortar and pestle until you get a yellow powder and add the hot water, and let it color the water. Add the salt, pepper, and cumin to the saffron mixture and pour it over the plum and chicken mixture. Add the chicken broth, cover, and simmer on very low heat for thirty minutes to an hour. You will know when the chicken is done when you cut a small piece from the thickest part and the middle is no longer pink. Serve on top of Bibi's Persian Saffron Rice.

Crush In The Time Of Cholera
Adas Polo or Lentil rice

I once bought a book not because I loved the author, Gabriel Garcia Marquez, but because the title really bemused me- Love In The Time of Cholera. It was fascinating to see two such opposing things placed side by side one another. I couldn't understand how the author had chosen to focus on love when there was such great turmoil surrounding it. But of all people, I should be the least surprised by this.

I was 17 when my world was turned upside down, and not in that fairytale kind of way; there was no prince finding my lost shoe or kissing me back to life after an eternity of sleep. In one day, the guardians of the revolution came to arrest my father, took us hostage all day, and then finally let us go only to trap him again later. My mother masterminded our escape from Iran with a group of shady smugglers who promised us the moon in Paris and delivered us to Kabul during the Soviet occupation. We were desperate, and so we saw value in anyone's promise.

My family crossed, or rather crawled, along the border to Afghanistan with many other refugees. We lived in large groups, inside houses that were confiscated from the previous regime in Afghanistan. Ours was house #4, formerly the home of one of the now overthrown Afghani king's brothers. The new government was friendly to us, and its people were in awe that my father, the poet, was now in their country. They gave us the nicest place they could. It looked like an upper middle class house in Tehran with gaudy décor. Each room was given to a few people, and all of us had nothing to do all day but wait for fate to take its course. We all managed to busy ourselves with something.

My something was a prominent journalist who'd crossed the border with my father when he had eventually come. He was in his early 40's, a handsome cross between Omar Sharif and Marcello Mastroianni, with a very positive and gregarious character. I knew him from very short past interactions when he visited my father at our house, but had never thought much of him. Now, far away from the bustle of the largest newspaper in Tehran, he set up a small news office in his bedroom for the newly formed group of immigrants, and used my brother and me as young journalists as we had very strong language skills. We listened to foreign language radios, and translated and transcribed the news for him. Even though it was a small task, at that time I felt I was helping in some major way.

The days were slow, so in between he would organize volleyball games in the garden, an escorted outing to the bazaar, or a painful viewing of a Soviet movie dubbed with a poor translation. He also happened to be a very good cook and even though the house already had one, he would sometimes go in the kitchen and make us something that reminded us of our homeland, always making sure to ask for my mother's opinion, of course.

I don't know what it was, perhaps it was just pure boredom, perhaps I let my imagination wander a little too far, but one day I realized that I was following him everywhere he went. A married man in Iran is like a forbidden item with a sold sticker pasted on him. His young family hadn't crossed the border yet, so he spent a lot of time with us and took a keen interest in me, one my teenage mind probably took a little too much to heart. He spent a lot of time with me talking about my future, about what was possible in this

25

new life I was headed for, and I think my parents were so depressed with our situation that they didn't even notice my infatuation. Looking back, I think what I really wanted was attention.

Months later, his family came and we all got settled in our own apartments. One day he came over with his Afghan driver and bodyguard to give me the news that my scholarship request to the Soviet Union that would allow me to go to school for journalism had been approved by the authorities. My mother wasn't home and she'd asked me that morning to prepare something for lunch. Even though he was in a hurry and the bodyguard was waiting, he taught me right then and there how to make Adas Polo- a lentil rice laced with rose petals, our magical advieh spices, and topped with caramelized onions, dates and raisins. When he left and my mother finally came home and tasted the dish, the first thing she said was, "You weren't home alone. There's no way you made this rice all by yourself." To this day, Adas Polo reminds me of my days filled with naïveté, innocence, hope and the endless possibilities of my teenage heart.

Adas Polo (Lentil Rice)

INGREDIENTS:

- 3 cups of jasmine Rice (with this method don't use basmati) for 1 cup of lentils, cooked with 2 cups of water al dente
- ½ tsp salt or more to taste
- 1 medium onion peeled and sliced (or buy fried onions if they are fried in vegetable oil)
- ½ cup olive oil
- ½ cup raisins
- 1 cup pitted dates, quartered
- 1 tsp ground saffron dissolved in 4 tbsp hot water
- ½ tsp ground cinnamon
- 1 tsp rose petals
- ¼ tsp cardamom
- ½ tsp cumin
- 1 tsp turmeric

PREPARATION:

Soak your lentils in one cup of water and bring it to a boil. Lower the heat until all the water is gone. Add your onion to it and mix (or you can wait and add the onions when you add the lentils to the rice-the order doesn't matter). Roast the dried and unwashed jasmine rice in olive oil for a few minutes until you notice a few yellow ones, and make sure they are all coated with olive oil. Flatten the rice and add water just enough to have an inch above the rice and salt it to your taste, i.e taste the water and if it tastes like well salted water then it's good. Add all the spices, half the saffron water and add the lentil and onion mix. Bring everything to a brisk boil on high heat and then lower and cover the pot, and don't open it. About 30 minutes later, open and form a mound with the rice towards the middle of the pot. Make some holes in the rice and add some slivers of butter (if you wish) to the top of the mound. Cover the lid with a kitchen towel if you wish to have a crust and let it go for another 20 minutes. Caramelize the dates and raisins with oil and or butter and add the other half of saffron water to it to garnish the top of the rice. You can add some caramelized onion to this mixture too. Plate it with raisins and dates on top and serve with Greek yogurt.

Sergei, the Drunk Soldier
Russian Borscht

Every now and then at around 1 or 2 am loud noises and fights awakened us in our dormitory hallway. It was never a question who the culprit was- it was always a man named Sergei. During the day, he was a shy, nice student with the stature of a body builder and he hardly made eye contact with anyone. At night though, it was a different story; he would turn into a drunk, cursing like a sailor and arguing with roommates over nothing. Depending on how he dressed, he could appear like a handsome soldier, or a rugged, unshaven mountain main. He also happened to be a fan of Sergei Visotski- the great Russian bard who chronicled the pain and suffering of his generation and whose songs were spread underground during the Soviet invasion.

One night, after one of these incidents, I couldn't go back to sleep and so I decided to go and talk to him and maybe even calm him down a little. He was so shaken up that he didn't even think twice about my strange request. I took him to the kitchen, wearing my robe and slippers, and he brought along his guitar. Sitting across from him I was repulsed by the overwhelming stench of his cigarette infused breath, but I didn't say anything. My family was still in Afghanistan, I hadn't made many friends, and sitting there in that kitchen a part of me just wanted to connect deeply with another human being.

I skipped the small talk and asked him where all his anger came from. As it turned out he had been a young soldier during the Afghan war and he proceeded to give me a chilling account of a time when he witnessed the Mujahidin burn his comrade alive. Consumed with anger, and not knowing what else to do, he had killed a few innocent children with his bare hands. I didn't know what to say to him. The image was brutal and such violence and suffering was unfamiliar to me. I couldn't grasp the exact feeling of how it must've been for him, and although my experiences were extremely different, I still wanted to share with him what I'd gone through before Moscow. I told him how I'd felt when the Iraqis bombed Tehran and we had to hide to in the basements, and how we fled Iran after the Islamic guards came to arrest my father. It wasn't the same experience, not by any means, and we came from different lands, but our shared grief and anger made me somehow feel like we had come from the same place.

As day started to break, our stomachs started to growl and Sergei offered to cook a borscht for us and to share his already made pirozhkis. The last time I'd had such treats was when I was in Iran and there was a big Russian colony that made and sold them. As it so happened, my new friend, the drunk Sergei, was a master of this piece of heaven on earth. The pirozhki is a soft, chewy dough that can be made with a savory or sweet custard filling. Borscht is the Russian's version of comfort food for cold days. He perfected the art of making them both, and also said that borscht was the best cure for a hangover. I only wish there was a recipe that could fix broken hearts and souls too.

Russian Borscht

INGREDIENTS:

- 2 large or 3 medium beets, thoroughly washed
- 2 large or 3 medium potatoes, sliced into bite-sized pieces
- 4 tbsp of cooking oil
- 1 medium onion, finely chopped
- 2 carrots, grated
- ½ head of cabbage, thinly chopped
- 1 can kidney beans with their water
- 2 bay leaves
- 6 tsp "Organic Better Than Bouillon Chicken Base" paste (this is equivalent to 6 cups of chicken broth. If using chicken broth, use 10 cups water and 6 cups broth)
- 5 tbsp ketchup (he used tomato paste but this is better)
- 4 tbsp lemon juice
- ¼ tsp freshly ground pepper
- 1 tbsp chopped dill for garnish
- Sour cream for garnish

PREPARATION:

Fill a large soup pot with 16 cups of water. Add 2 – 3 beets. Cover and boil for about 1 hour. Once you can smoothly pierce the beets with a butter knife, remove from the water and set aside to cool. Keep the water. Slice 3 potatoes, add into the same water and boil 15-20 minutes. Grate both carrots and dice one onion. Add 4 Tbsp of cooking oil to the skillet and sauté vegetables until they are soft. Stir in ketchup when they are almost done cooking. Thinly shred ½ a cabbage and add it to the pot when potatoes are half way done. Next, peel and slice the beets into matchsticks and add them back to the pot. Add Bouillon paste, lemon juice, pepper, bay leaves and can of kidney beans (with their water) to the pot. Add sautéed carrots and onion to the pot along with chopped dill. Cook for another 5-10 minutes, until the cabbage is done. Serve with a dollop of sour cream, diced dill, and a piece of pirozhki.

Fighting or Feasting
Chicken Tagine with Medjool Dates

One night, I heard the sound of a brawl coming from the end of the corridor that led to the communal kitchen. Curious as ever, because it wasn't the sound of Sergei's Russian I was hearing, and a savvy mediator by now in the art of ending student fights, I walked over to see what was going on. To my surprise it wasn't a brawl at all, but a culinary feast. The Moroccan students were back from a visit home with a ton of local ingredients and since they were apparently jetlagged they'd decided to throw a feast.

They welcomed me to join and I gladly inhaled all the familiar scents and forgot about sleep. They call it raas al hanoot, we call it advieh and the Indians call it curry- basically a blend of Eastern spices they were using to bring their food to life. They argued about which local tribes cooked the best dishes, and it reminded me of Iran and how every section of the country is known for making a specific kind of dish, and how someone outside of this area could never be considered an expert. Laughter mixed with their stern protests. Deep down everyone knew who cooked it best was an argument no one could ever win.

That night I learned that their famous tagine is exactly the same as the Persian khoresh with a few twists and turns. They use a beautiful clay dish to cook the braise, and serve it on top of couscous instead of rice. As I closed my eyes to taste the first spoonful of this delightful food, I was transported back to the palm deserts of the south of Iran with their bountiful dates. Inside this tagine from the south of Morocco, there was a heavenly piece of nature's finest sweetness-dates, mingled with chicken, spices, sauces that are too varied and powerful to describe, but easy enough to make. Although no one outside of Morocco will probably ever be considered the best at making this dish, it's certainly worth a try.

Chicken Tagine with Medjool dates

INGREDIENTS:

- 3 1/2 lbs chicken breast halves, thighs or drumsticks
- 2 tbsp all purpose flour
- 1 tbsp extra-virgin olive oil
- 2 lbs shallots (about 9 large), peeled and diced
- 3 cinnamon sticks
- 1 1/2 tsp ground ginger
- 1 tsp ground cumin
- 1/2 tsp turmeric
- 1/8 tsp cayenne pepper
- 3 cups low-salt chicken broth
- 5 tbsp fresh lemon juice, divided
- 12 dates, pitted, halved
- 1/4 cup almonds, toasted, coarsely chopped
- 1/4 cup chopped fresh cilantro

PREPARATION:

Sprinkle chicken pieces with salt, pepper, and flour. Heat olive oil in heavy large pot over medium-high heat. Add half of the chicken pieces to pot and cook until browned on all sides, turning occasionally, about 15 minutes. Transfer chicken to baking sheet or platter; repeat with remaining chicken. Pour off all but 2 tablespoons fat from pot and discard. Reduce heat to medium. Add shallots to pot; sauté until golden, for about 6 minutes. Add cinnamon sticks, ginger, cumin, turmeric, and cayenne. Stir until fragrant, about 1 minute. Increase heat to high; add broth and 3 tablespoons lemon juice. Bring to boil, reduce heat to low, cover, and simmer until shallots begin to soften, about 18 minutes. Place chicken pieces atop shallots in the pot. Bring to boil over medium heat. Reduce heat to medium-low, cover, and simmer until juices run clear when thickest part of drumstick is pierced with knife, about 25 minutes. Transfer chicken and shallots to the platter and tent with foil. Boil juices in pot until slightly thickened. Stir in dates and remaining 2 tablespoons lemon juice. Reduce heat and simmer gently until dates are heated through, about 2 minutes. Pour sauce and dates over chicken. Sprinkle with almonds and cilantro, and serve over couscous.

Food that Lifts You Up
Chana Bateta

I've never been to India, but I have been to a Diwali party, which is the festival of lights, and really the greatest time to taste some real homemade Indian food. In Moscow ingredients were obviously limited, so it was more like a makeshift Diwali party, but it was the first time I'd actually tried Indian food and my taste buds had never been happier. It was like Persian food, but actually spicy.

My Indian girlfriends knew how much I loved food and cooking, and were kind enough to invite me to the pre-party, which was a gathering of only women before all of the guests arrived. My family was still in Afghanistan and I hadn't seen them in so long, so when I entered that noisy, potent, chaotic kitchen I felt so relieved. This is how my aunts would prepare for a dinner party; all the women, young and old, stuffed into the kitchen,

chopping and stirring and gossiping away. These women welcomed me with open arms and put me right to work. A few of them sat in the corner threading each other's eyebrows, one woman told a story about how she first fell in love, laughter bounced through the kitchen and my heart felt suddenly lifted.

I won't dare encapsulate the great depth and length of Indian cuisine here because the subcontinent is big and the traditions so varied that you can have a dish in North India and then have something else in the south and think that these two dishes are indeed from two different continents. However, I'd like to honor Indian cuisine and the great tradition of Ayurvedic cuisine by giving you some of my favorite dishes that I call comfort food for rainy days. Trust me when I say there's no problem the right food can't fix.

Chana Bateta

INGREDIENTS:

- ½-1 cup diced tomatoes
- 1 tbsp tomato paste
- 1 1/2 tbsp vegetable oil
- 1/2 tsp mustard seeds (black or brown, not yellow)
- 2 shallots, sliced
- 3 large cloves garlic, minced
- 1 tbsp minced ginger
- 1 tsp cumin
- 1 1/2 tsp coriander
- 1/4 tsp cayenne, or more to taste
- 1/3 to 1/2 cup coconut milk
- 1 tsp salt
- 1 tsp sugar
- 1 or 2 large Yukon Gold potatoes cut into approximate 1 1/2" dice
- 1 can chickpeas
- 2 tbsp finely chopped cilantro, plus a few sprigs for garnish

PREPARATION:

Combine the diced tomatoes and tomato paste in a mini food processor and process until smooth. Set aside. Heat the oil over high heat in a large cast iron pan until smoking. Add the mustard seeds and cover immediately, and wait till they stop popping (15 seconds). Turn the heat to medium and add the shallots, garlic, and ginger. Cook for about 5 minutes, stirring nearly constantly, until the shallots are quite golden. Add the cumin, coriander, and cayenne, and cook for another minute or so, to toast the spices. Pour in the pureed tomato, and cook down for 3-4 minutes. It should be reduced to an almost paste-like consistency. Pour in the coconut milk and the salt and sugar and bring to a boil. Add the potatoes and return to a boil, then turn the heat to low and cover the pan. Cook until the potatoes are soft--easily pierced with a knife--then uncover and add the chickpeas with some of the liquid from the can. Cook for 5 or 10 minutes, until heated through. Add the cilantro and cook a minute more. Serve over rice or naan.

New Year's Eve in a Crowded Moscow Dorm Room
Khoresh Gheimeh Bademjan

One New Year's Eve in Moscow, my Afghani girlfriend Najiba and I had nowhere to go. Most students deserted the dorms between Dec 20th and Jan 10th to be with their families. So only "orphans" like us would stay behind. Most of my friends were from civilized countries and had no problem going back, but that wasn't the case for us. Feeling nostalgic for our war-torn countries and our families, we decided to prepare some food that would remind us of home. Najiba and I barely talked, we were so focused on our cooking, but soon our Iraqi friend interrupted us asking what we were doing. We explained to him our plan, and he insisted that the kitchen was no place for anyone to spend the last night of the year, especially not two beautiful girls like us. He invited us to his room where

they were celebrating New Years Eve in style.

Despite what you've heard in the news about Iran and Iraq, Iraqi people love Iranian women. They think Persian girls are straight out of Scheherazade's 1001 Nights. As soon as we entered the room, the conversation got louder and eyes fixated on us, but we couldn't understand a word since neither Najiba nor I spoke Arabic. We realized that there are only a few other girls in the room, and the way these boys looked at us it was as if God had sent us to them as a last minute New Year's gift. As they got ready to bring the food from the kitchen, we offered to bring our food and they welcomed the idea. We broke bread and they showered us with kindness and generosity and made us feel so welcome. We compared notes about

our dishes and in what ways they were similar or different. I tried shawerma, kibba, and falafel for the first time. I was familiar with hummus and tabouleh already. I'd made Khoresh Gheimeh Bademjan and they were flabbergasted to learn that I made it with beef and not lamb. I explained that I didn't like the muttony flavor of lamb and they teased me that despite my appearances, I must not really be Persian.

We drank, we sang, we danced. We ate and for a moment in time we were all brothers and sisters far away from the tanks, guns, missiles and wars in which our countrymen were fighting. This is the magic spell that good food puts on all of us; we forget the pain of the past for a second and are able to be in the moment, with the flavor and tastes that bring joy to our bellies, the faces and their kindness that warm our hearts.

Khoresh Gheimeh Bademjan

INGREDIENTS:

- 1 lb beef, extra fat trimmed, cut into ½ inch cubes
- ½ cup split peas
- 3 cups thinly sliced onions
- 3 ½ tbsp minced garlic
- 2 tbsp tomato paste
- 5 whole dried Persian limes, pierced
- 1 ½ tsp freshly ground black pepper
- 2 tsp salt
- 1 tbsp turmeric plus ¼ Tsp for peas
- ½ tsp ground saffron threads
- 1 tsp rose petals
- ½ tsp cinnamon
- ½ tsp cumin
- 3 ½ cups water
- 8 Chinese eggplants, or 2 Italian eggplants, peeled and cut lengthwise.

PREPARATION:

In a non-stick pot, lightly brown the onions in 6 tbsp oil, over medium-high heat. Add meat, salt, and pepper, stirring occasionally until onions and meat are brown. Add garlic and 1 tbsp turmeric. Stir for 2 more minutes. Pour in 3 ½ cups water and dried Persian limes. Cover and bring to a boil. Then reduce the heat to low and cook for 1 hour. Meanwhile in a small nonstick pot, cook yellow split peas in 1 cup of water, ¼ tsp salt, and ¼ tsp turmeric, over low heat, for 15 minutes or until tender. Drain in colander and set aside. In another deep pan, add oil and sauté eggplants until golden brown. Add tomato paste, cumin, saffron, rose petals, and cinnamon to the pot. Layer the eggplant over the stew. Cover and simmer over low heat for another 45 minutes. Check if meat is tender. Adjust the seasoning to taste. Add cooked split peas to the pot. Cover and simmer for 5 more minutes. Transfer the khoresh into a shallow serving dish. Serve with fluffy, steamed, saffron rice.

How to Eat Like Royalty
Bahn Mi Sandwiches

I didn't know much about Vietnamese people before Moscow. Each year the Republic of Vietnam sent thousands of students to the Soviet Union to train their next generation of officers. It was normal to see many students from Vietnam. The Soviets had extensive language training, but the Asian students had the toughest time learning Russian. The Vietnamese students, although very studious and precocious, were challenged by the language, and so were isolated mostly because nobody could understand them. They were constantly made fun of for their looks, how they smelled, and everyone said they spoke like cats.

I didn't know what to believe, but once I saw the colorful and beautiful dishes they cooked, I knew there had to be a great culture behind these quiet people. I tried to communicate with them by asking easy and friendly questions, and sometimes even pretended to understand. They were naturally expert cooks and since they traveled to their country more than once a year, they brought a lot of their food back with them. They were kind enough to offer me their rolls, sauces and famous Pho soup, but what impressed me the most was a sandwich that I later learned the correct name for- Bahn Mi.

It was simple enough to make, elegant, delicious and filled you up for a busy and cold day on the run. No matter how much they were teased though, as soon as they opened their neatly foiled sandwiches for lunch, they suddenly turned into kings and queens who everyone envied. That's the power of food- it can turn a cat into a king.

Caramelized Pork Bánh Mì

INGREDIENTS:

- 1 lb pork tenderloin
- 3 tbsp fish sauce
- 2 tbsp maple syrup
- 1 tbsp brown sugar
- 2 tbsp soy sauce
- 1/2 tsp sesame oil
- 2 garlic cloves, minced
- 1 slice ginger, minced
- 1 green onion, sliced thinly
- 1/2 tsp black pepper
- 2 tbsp vegetable oil
- 1 loaf sweet French baguette with a crisp crust and tender center
- Lettuce
- Pickled carrot and radishes
- Thinly sliced jalapeno chili peppers
- Cilantro
- Pâté (optional)
- Mayonnaise

Pickled Carrots and Radishes

- 1/4 pound baby carrots, peeled (I like to peel them with a hand peeler very thin)
- 1 bunch red radishes or daikon, which is more traditional
- 1/2 cup water
- 1 cup apple cider or white vinegar
- 1 tbsp salt
- 2 tbsp sugar

Slice carrots and radishes into quarters lengthwise. Mix all ingredients together. Let stand as little as an hour or as long as overnight.

PREPARATION:

Cut tenderloin across the grain of the meat into ½ inch pieces. Flatten each piece to an even ¼ inch between two pieces of saran wrap using a meat pounder or the back of your pan. Mix ingredients from fish sauce to black pepper. It should be sweet and savory so add more soy sauce, salt, or sesame oil as you like. Add marinade to the meat and make sure all pieces of meat are coated. Marinate for 10-30 minutes. You can cook the pork on the grill outdoors or indoors using a hot grill pan or cast iron pan. Add vegetable oil to meat and stir to coat. Sear first side of meat until very dark brown on one side, then flip and sear on the second side. Be careful not to overcook it. The meat is thin so it cooks quickly, one or two minutes on each side. To assemble sandwiches, slice baguette and spread mayonnaise on one side, pâté on the other. Add lettuce, meat, pickled vegetables, cilantro and peppers.

Mourning For Love The Western Way
Makowiec

In the dorms I was stuck rooming with a Polish girl who refused to speak Russian with me because she hated Russians. I spoke six languages at the time, but Polish wasn't one of them. I couldn't stand the silence in our room though, so I started taking Polish lessons. We couldn't have been more opposite; she was narcissistic, overly sexual, and I was more naïve than I'd like to admit. At times I was in awe of her, especially when it came to men and how easy it was for her to drop one and move on to the next.

I had a boyfriend then and I was certain we were in love, only to have him break up with me after a few months. I sat in my room crying over it one day when my roommate walked in, and to my surprise asked me what was wrong. I told her what had happened and she shrugged it off like it was no big deal at all. A few days later she walked into the room and I was in the same position, still crying. She asked me what was wrong again. I told her again that I'd broken up with my boyfriend, and her eyes widened in shock.

"You're still crying from that? I see you are suffering the Eastern way and I am doing it the Western way."

"What's the Western way?" I asked her through my tears.

"You cry for ten minutes, and then you go find someone new." We both laughed at this, and for the first time I felt like I could actually learn something from this girl.

Although we had our differences, she knew my love for food and when she'd come back from a trip from Poland she'd share the food her mother

had cooked for her. I'll never forget the smoked Kielbasa and
the poppy seeds rolls. I tried
later in life to replicate the
rolls and here is the best I
could come up with- you
may get high if you have
too much, so be careful!

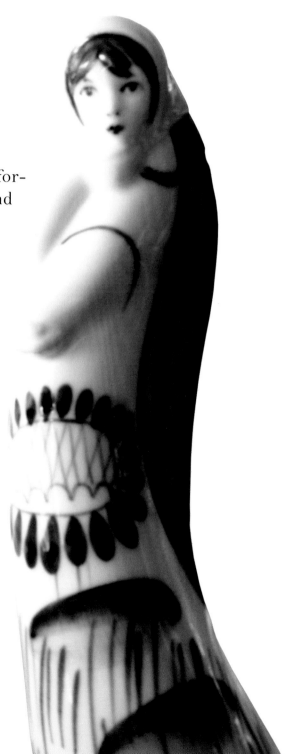

Makowiec

INGREDIENTS:

Canned poppy seed paste available in the ethnic aisle of most supermarkets can be used, but directions are also given if you choose to make your own filling.

- **1 package active dry yeast**
- **2 cups warm milk**
- **8 cups all-purpose flour**
- **3/4 cup sugar**
- **1 tsp salt**
- **5 eggs**
- **4 oz (1 stick) butter, melted**
- **2 (11-oz) cans poppy seed filling (or make your own, see below)**

Filling Ingredients:

- **1lb ground poppy seeds**
- **1 cup sugar**
- **6 oz softened butter (1 1/2 sticks)**
- **1 cup hot milk**
- **1 lemon rind, grated**

PREPARATION:

If making your own filling, grind the poppy seeds in a grinder then combine all filling ingredients. Beat well and set aside. In a small heatproof bowl, dissolve yeast in 1/2 cup of the warm milk. In the bowl of a stand mixer or a large bowl, combine flour, sugar, salt and eggs. Add remaining 1 1/2 cups warm milk, butter and yeast mixture. With the paddle attachment, or by hand, beat until smooth. Dough will be sticky at this point. Scrape dough into a clean, greased bowl. Sprinkle the top with a little flour and cover. Let stand in a warm place for 1 hour or until double in size. Punch down dough and turn out onto a floured surface. Divide dough in half and shape each half into a rectangle. Spread 1 can or half of the filling you made on each rectangle of dough and roll up like a jellyroll. Turn ends under so filling will not leak out. Place on a parchment-lined or greased pan, cover and let rise again until double in size. Heat oven to 350 degrees. Brush tops of rolls with additional melted butter. Bake 45 to 60 minutes or until rolls are golden brown. Remove from oven and cool. Dust rolls with confectioner's sugar, if desired.

When I was 13 years old it was hard to understand what the wrinkly fortuneteller explained to me. *Men will always find you attractive and mysterious. Your life will be filled with turmoil. You will live most of your life outside your birthplace.* I was at a hair salon with my aunt and she was reading fortunes for some ladies from the grinds of Turkish coffee and I begged her to read mine while my aunt was getting her hair done. I expected happy things, a joyful destiny, but everything that came out of her mouth made me feel as if my life was doomed.

In 1989 my married Lithuanian friend Yolita wanted to get rid of a Japanese guy who was after her so in her infinite wisdom she invited me to a Japanese tea party that this businessman was hosting in his very plush apartment in the most luxurious hotel in Moscow. Of course she didn't tell me what her agenda was.

In turn, I invited Najiba with me and I took the great initiative to dress in Japanese Kimono as a way of honoring our host for inviting us to our first Japanese tea party.

As the door opened, his jaw dropped. He couldn't believe that Najiba and I were wearing Kimonos. He was so happy that he did his best tea presentation and then insisted on us staying and he made the most beautiful sushi rolls. This was the first time I ever had sushi-raw fish on top of rice that looked unlike our delectable Persian rice. While my two other friends wanted to puke, I enjoyed every bite of it and with each bite Mizuki became fonder of me. He was the most handsome Asian man I've ever met to this day. He was tall and slender with long fingers and a great sense of fashion. He was soft spoken and very diplomatic, but unfortunately not my type.

We went to his house for dinner a few nights after that and one time dinner took longer than ever, and he gave me a ride home because it was way below zero outside. Right at our apartment door, and before dropping me off, he casually gave me a box out of the dashboard. I looked at him and something felt wrong. My heart started beating funny. He insisted that I open the box, and when I did what looked back at me was beyond shocking- it was a diamond ring.

Apparently he'd been reading too much into our friendship. When I told him I couldn't accept the ring he threatened suicide. I jumped out of the car, ran upstairs and woke my father and told him someone was going to commit suicide downstairs. My parents had been evacuated to Moscow right after the Red Army left Afghanistan, three years after I'd come, and we were living together at the time. My father reassured me that no one was going to kill himself. Then he took me to the window on the fourth floor and he told me to look down.

"You see? He's still alive and waiting for you," my father said.

"He's waiting to kill himself."

"Let him. If he really tries to kill himself then I would say you should marry him and we will have to suffer all of our lives eating that raw fish on top of bad rice. " My father, a romantic poet, well versed in the tales of Khosrow and Shirin, Layla and Majnun knew well that few people in this life would kill themselves for love. The words of the fortuneteller rang like bells in my ear that night. My life has certainly not been doomed, but I've always attracted strange and emotional men. I never saw Mizuki after that night, but my love for sushi has certainly never left me.

61

Bibi's California Roll

INGREDIENTS:

- 3 cups white Japanese sushi rice
- 3 cups water
- 1/4 cup mirin, plus additional for moistening nori
- 2 tbsp sugar
- 1 3-inch piece of Dashi Konbu (kelp to give taste to the rice)
- 5 sheets nori (1 package)
- 1 carrot, julienned
- 1 avocado sliced
- 1 scallion, julienned (green part only)
- 1 hothouse cucumber, seeded and julienned
- A mixture of cream cheese or mayo and Sriracha sauce
- Light soy sauce
- Sesame Seeds (optional)

PREPARATION:

Place the rice in a bowl and rinse under cold running water until the water is fairly clear, about 5 minutes. Shake the water out and allow the rice to dry in the strainer for a few minutes. Put the rice in a pot with exactly 3 cups of water and cook covered with the dashi konbu inside over high heat until it starts to foam, about 5 minutes. Reduce the heat to low and cook until tender, about 15 minutes. Turn off the heat and sprinkle with 1/4 cup mirin, with the sugar already dissolved in it. Replace the lid and allow the rice to steam for 15 minutes then take out the kelp. Place in a wooden bowl and cool to room temperature using a fan.

To prepare the sushi, place a bamboo sushi roller flat on a table with the bamboo reeds horizontal to you. Cover with sheet of plastic wrap. Place 1 nori sheet on top, smooth side down, and moisten lightly with mirin, or water. With damp hands, press 1 1/4 cups rice flat on top of the nori, leaving 1 1/2-inch edges on the top and bottom, but pressing all the way to the sides. Make sure the rice is pressed even and smooth. Then spread some cream cheese, or the mayo, and Sriracha mixture all over the rice. Place strips of carrots horizontally on top and follow by piling the avocados, scallions, and cucumbers on top, making a tight, straight bundle of vegetables. Place 1 layer of pickled ginger slices on top (optional).

To roll the sushi, pick up near the edge of the bamboo roller and hold it with the nori. Then, pull them up and over the vegetable bundle until the nori reaches the rice on the other side. Press the roller to make a round bundle, then roll the bundle to the far edge of the nori and press again to make a round bundle. The nori should totally enclose the rice and vegetables in a round tube, but the ends will have rice and vegetables sticking out. Repeat the process with the remaining ingredients. To serve, slice off the ends with a very sharp knife and slice each roll into 8 equal pieces and sprinkle with white or black sesame seeds. Serve the sushi at room temperature with the soy sauce and wasabi. You can use crab or imitation crab and the mayo and Sriracha mixture to make it non- vegetarian.

You Are Worthy
Far Breton

I was supposed to get married to a Frenchman who took great pride in being from Brittany, where of course he thought food was the best in the world. How an Iranian woman like myself could accept this belief is another story, which perhaps is why we never tied the knot.

On my first trip to Brittany with my Frenchman to meet his family, I was made to taste all the delectable treats of the region. I have to say, I was impressed, and had an extra ten pounds afterwards to show for it. To this day, I have lovely memories of Kouing Aman, a premium type of croissant which is sweet and a bit salty at the same time, Galettes Bretonnes that are much better than their northern neighbor's short bread cookies, and the huge savory crepes Bretons made of whole wheat, stuffed with a great ham and egg omelet.

In a region that boasts such pride in the native cuisine, it should've been no surprise to me that what would make the biggest impression on my mother-in-law to be wasn't when I spoke French like a native, but the day I demonstrated to her my culinary prowess in the kitchen. She was impressed by my stews, and like most people the crispy part of the rice I made. Recognizing me as worthy, she then shared with me her tour de force in the form of Far Breton and even went so far as to give me the recipe. As it turns out, it was her son's favorite thing to eat so I'm sure there was a hidden message buried in there somewhere, an expectation that I'd cook it for him every day. Far Breton is a custardy pudding cake, similar to a clafouti but with a dense, smooth, flan-like texture punctuated with delicate prunes. Her secret to success was soaking the prunes in cognac, which results in a je ne sais quoi taste. The Bretons eat their Far as breakfast as well as dessert and I must say- C'est parfait! Things didn't work out with the Frenchman, as it turned out I was luckier when it came to cooking.

Far Breton

INGREDIENTS:

- 3 eggs, room temperature

- ½ cup sugar

- ¾ cup flour

- 2 cups whole milk, room temperature

- 4 tbsp butter

- Pinch of salt

- 10 to 15 prunes, soaked in cognac for 20 min (optional)

PREPARATION

Preheat your oven at 350 for 15 minutes. Mix in order the eggs, the sugar, the flour and salt until you have a homogenous batter. Then add the milk little by little while whisking. Butter a Pyrex generously with the butter and add the batter to the dish. Add the prunes at the end. You can also try raisins, cherries and apricots. Then place the dish in the oven at 375 degrees for 45 minutes to an hour until you see the golden brown top. Cool it and place it in the fridge then serve.

Something Out of Nothing
Pineapple Flambé

I learned English watching Lucille Ball and Oprah Winfrey. Years after arriving in Moscow I was finally granted a student visa to come to the United States. I lived with my mom's cousin Shokooh and her family in Washington D.C. and without much money, stayed home and watched television so my English could improve. I made hundreds of copies of my resume and sent them to every company that existed in D.C., my dream all the while being to work at the World Bank. I scheduled a lunch with a friend of mine who worked there one day and brought a stack of freshly printed resumes with me. She called me crazy, told me that there were no openings and the only way you could even get hired was if you had a connection. After lunch I strolled through the parking lot, stuffing my resume in between the windshield wipers of the most expensive cars, who I knew were most likely the executives. This is how I landed my first job in America at The World Bank. I moved out of Shokooh's home because it was too far and I didn't have a car, and I ended up renting a room in my French-speaking colleague's home who also offered to drive me to work. She was a great improvisational cook, and like me loved to share with others. One night, my friends and I arrived home after a long night of partying and dancing and sat down to talk to her. We weren't hungry, but all wanted something sweet. There was nothing open at that time so she offered to make dessert. "Are you crazy? You want to bake at this ungodly hour?" I asked, but she smiled in that all-knowing way a cook does when she has a plan and grabbed a skillet, a few bananas, some Kahlua, and whipped a great sauce to go on top of vanilla ice cream. I had to stop my friends from

licking their plates clean. When I think of this night, it makes me realize that the mark of a great cook is the ability to adapt, to be creative, and quite possibly to turn what appears to be nothing into something delicious. Years later inspired by this moment I decided to take it a notch up and came up with my own signature dessert that I call Pineapple Flambé. I opened a can of pineapple, I added a few flakes of coconut and YES cracked pepper on top and voila, something out of nothing!

Pineapple Flambé

INGREDIENTS:

- 1 pineapple, cleaned, cut and cored

- ¼ cup Kahlua

- Ice cream

- Cracked pepper

- ¼ cup butter

- Coconut powder or cracked amaretti biscottis (optional)

PREPARATION

Cut the pineapples and core them. Sauté them on both sides in 1/4 cup butter. Sprinkle ground black pepper on top and add 1/4 cup of Kahlua. You may want to sprinkle some coconut powder or crush a few amaretti biscottis on top of the ice cream and garnish with a piece of mint. Then, take a spoonful of the sauce from the bottom of the pan and spread on the ice cream.

ادویه باز

در روزی از روزهای دوران تمرین نمایش مهره‌ی سُرخ، مهمان بی بی کسرایی بودیم و او مشغول پخت خوراک. بی بی با مهارت و ذوق، ادویه‌های معطر و رنگارنگ را با دست روی غذا می‌پاشید.

72

مُلاعبه و عشق بازی بی بی با غذا همراه با حرکات دوار دستش مرا یاد حرکت خطوط ظریف و دوار مینیاتور ایرانی انداخت. به یکباره گفتم تو ادویه بازی...! واو به راستی ادویه بازاست.

...پخت غذای خوب، تنها به تغذیه‌ی انسان مربوط نیست که با روح و عاطفه هم در ارتباط است. غذایی که با شتاب پخته شود از آن بوی بی حوصلگی به مشام می‌رسد.

آگاهی از فرهنگ و لذت آشپزی، تمرکز در سختن، توجه به تنوع، رنگ آمیزی، طعم، بو، تزئینات غذا، همه و همه عواملی است که انرژی مثبت، عشق و محبّت را همراه با غذا منتقل می‌کنند که بی تردید عشق به غذا طعم می دهد و آشپزی با طعم عشق، نشان از مهارت و عشق استاد ادویه باز است.

گردآفرید

The Replicator
Pad Thai

The first time I went to Thailand with my husband at the time, I thought I'd found heaven on earth. I've seen many beautiful places, but not many towns with such stunning, respectful, and peaceful people. I think it's a mixture of the majestic scenery, the unique food, and the calm of their ancient Buddhist beliefs. It's rare that you travel to another country as a tourist and find that locals are nice to you not because you're paying them for food or a room, but because this is simply who they are.

My ex-husband used to call me "The Replicator" because wherever we went, he'd put something he'd really liked in my mouth and would ask if I could make it for him once we got home. Generally, I could guess all the ingredients and deliver the desired dish. But, I must confess that I was totally lost with

Thai flavors and scents. I really had to study and learn the different ingredients, spices, and herbs that were completely foreign to me. The alchemy of ingredients was also fascinating to me. The first time I actually smelled fish sauce I though it was the most disgusting thing on earth, but once put into a soup it changed into something magical.

The food is simple enough that I once saw a woman making Pad Thai on her little boat with one hand while paddling with the other hand. Yet, this same food is sophisticated enough that you can serve it for an elaborate, thoughtful dinner. I promise you won't have too much trouble making this, just make sure to use both hands.

Pad Thai with Tofu

INGREDIENTS:
For the sauce:
- ½ cup tamarind concentrate or paste
- 1/3 cup palm sugar
- ¼ cup fish sauce
- 2 tbsp sambal oelek
- 1 tbsp oyster sauce

For the Pad Thai:
- 1 pack of rice noodles for pad thai
- 2 tbsp canola oil
- 3 scallions, thinly sliced
- 1 tbsp minced garlic
- 1 diced shallot
- 3 beaten eggs
- 1 box of firm tofu, cubed (you can also use finely chopped chicken tenders)
- 1 cup shredded carrots
- 1 cup fresh bean sprouts
- Chopped roasted peanuts
- Chopped fresh cilantro
- Lime wedges

PREPARATION:

In a pan simmer the sugar, the tamarind sauce, the fish sauce, the oyster sauce and sambal oelek for a few minutes and set aside. For the Pad Thai: soak the noodles in hot water until soft and pliable and drain and set aside. Heat in a skillet over medium high 1 tbsp of oil, add the shallots and garlic until a bit brown, about 2-4 minutes. Add the carrots and tofu, and sear then add the eggs and the noodles and the sauce and let it absorb for 4-5 minutes. After you stir everything you can garnish with the peanuts, bean sprouts, cilantro and lime wedges.

The Rice Rules
Persian Jasmine Rice

Every Iranian woman will judge whether someone is a good cook or not based on how well his or her rice turns out. If it's too wet, it means the cook was impatient. If it's too oily, the cook was obviously careless. Rice plays a critical role in every Persian meal, not only for sopping up sauces and giving them texture, but also as a carbohydrate that gives sustenance throughout the day to rich and poor alike. Basmati rice, the kind Iranians usually use, is light, fluffy, elongated and dances when cooked with a generous amount of oil. It can be dressed up or dressed down; served at the simplest of family dinners or the grandest of weddings. However, most anyone would agree that the very best part of a pot of Persian rice is the crusty bottom, or tahdig, literally meaning "bottom of the pot". If your rice comes out perfectly, but your tah-dig is burnt or not crisp enough, your cooking skills would still be questionable.

I haven't yet met a person in my life who's tasted Persian rice and the tahdig and hasn't loved it, but achieving a perfect bottom crust in the classic Persian method is no easy task because it takes a long time just to make the rice. In the traditional method, the basmati rice is first soaked in water with rock salt, then a pot of water is brought to a boil and the pre-soaked rice is added and boiled, then drained, and the drained rice is then lightly toasted in oil, before it's steamed once again. Finally, the rice is done and it's covered with a dry cloth on top to create the perfect crust. Just describing the process is tiring enough.

I love Persian rice and tahdig, but I knew there had to be an easier solution that would allow my family and me to enjoy this rice every day without sacrificing our entire day preparing it. The answer lay in swapping out the basmati rice, which originates in India and is a drier rice that requires a lot of water, and replacing it with the equally lovely Thai jasmine rice. Jasmine rice grains are not quite as narrow and elongated

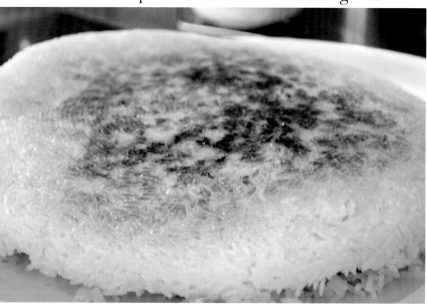

as basmati and so some purists think that jasmine can't possibly do the trick, but Bibi's Persian Jasmine Rice results in the same light, fluffy rice dish as the original. By eliminating the repetitive tasks of soaking and boiling, the focus can be on achieving the perfect finishing touch, the crust.

My mother, on the other hand, wasn't so convinced. The first time I introduced this idea to her she was visiting me in San Diego from Vienna and thought it is was blasphemy. She quite calmly told me that now that I had a cooking school I had a reputation to uphold. She didn't want others making fun of me for screwing up this classically simple dish. She's a wonderful cook, one women call for recipes, so her words carry a lot of weight, but I asked her to eat my rice with an open mind. The entire time I was making it though, she was rolling her eyes, huffing and puffing, all the while exclaiming that she was keeping an open mind. That's the thing about having two cooks in the kitchen; both believe that their way is the best way. Despite our differences, when I finally unveiled the rice the first words out of her mouth were- This smells so good! Her pride couldn't even let her deny it. When she tasted her first spoon she asked me where I thought she could buy jasmine rice in Vienna.

The Rice Rules

Bibi's Persian Jasmine Rice

INGREDIENTS:

- **2 tbsp olive or canola oil**

- **2 cups jasmine rice**

- **1 clove of garlic (optional)**

- **3 ½ cups water or about a knuckle of water above the flattened rice**

- **2 tsp kosher salt**

- **Saffron (optional)**

- **3 tsp butter cut into small rectangles**

PREPARATION:

In a medium nonstick saucepan heat the oil over high heat. Add the rice and a clove of garlic and cook, stirring frequently, until a few grains of rice turn golden blonde, or for about 6 to 7 minutes. Immediately add water, it should be enough to cover the rice and about one inch of water above the rice. Salt the water and add the saffron. Bring the mixture to a brisk boil. Cover and reduce the heat to medium-low and let it simmer for 20 to 25 minutes until the rice is tender and all the liquid is absorbed. Remove the garlic clove before serving.

Tahdig :

If you wish to have the crust on the bottom you must stop the steaming. In order to do so, open the pot and mound the rice and make 6 or 7 holes with the end of your spatula throughout the pot and add small pieces of cut butter inside the holes. Place a kitchen towel over the top of the pan, replace the lid and cover it tightly. Cook again for another 30-45 minutes on medium heat. Remove the pan from the heat and serve.

The Half Human
Pasta Spontanea

We've traveled so far together, and now our journey finally brings us to Harvard Cookin' Girl. I was in the store one day minding my business when a dapper young man with European mannerisms walked in and introduced himself to me. His name was Marko Dedic. I immediately suspected a Slavic accent and a Serbian name and asked him if he was Serbian. He responded with a smirk on his face, "Yes I am half Serbian," he said. I asked what the other half was and he replied, "Human." I knew at that moment that someone with a great sense of humor had walked into my kitchen, and yes half a human being better than most whole ones. Marko had also experienced a challenging journey to come to America, and he also had a true passion for food and the kind of generosity that's indispensable if you're a man who likes to feed others. He's the Maitre D' at one of the most prestigious restaurants in San Diego, but in reality he has what it takes to be the chef of his own restaurant. Together we've brainstormed some of the most amazing events at Harvard Cookin' Girl because he understands people; he's a storyteller and most of all he knows his food.

There's no need for him to do this for a living, but he shows up at my school with joy and excitement, always ready to cook. Over time and through our shared love of food and similar backgrounds I've forged yet another friendship, and have welcomed another member into my tribe. I've learned so much from him about the simplicity of good food.

One day, the kids at the studio wanted pasta with bacon sauce and we didn't have any of the ingredients, so he created a spontaneous meal for all of us that satisfied kids and adults and spurred the idea of our "Spontaneous Mondays". I'd like to share

the recipe here, as Marko himself has writ-ten it, so you can not only enjoy the pas-ta, but so you can also have a taste of who Marko really is.

Pasta Spontanea

The Sauce

INGREDIENTS:

- 1 leek

- 1 Cup sweet peas

- 6 heads of shiitake or porcini mushrooms

- 2 tsp Italian parsley, diced

- Sea salt

- Black pepper

- 2-3 tbsp Olive oil

- Fresh pasta, but if you don't have a market where you can get fresh pasta use dry pasta

PREPARATION:

Hello pasta lovers! Here is a simple spring pasta recipe that would make your mouth water every time you make it. It's a very seasonal recipe and a wonderful lunch idea.

Of course fresh pasta is a must, but if you don't have a market where you can get fresh pasta use dry instead and follow the direction on the box. The difference is in cooking them, since fresh will cook only for a minute or so and dry would have to be cooked for 9 minutes for Al Dente. Let's first start with 2 tablespoons of olive oil in a medium sauté pan. Slice leeks and mushrooms (not chopped) julienne style. Start sautéing leeks first just until they are fragrant and almost soft, then add the mushrooms and continue sautéing on medium heat until translucent. In the same time steame or boil the peas for 45 seconds and once done, add in the pan with mushrooms and leeks. Now it's time to season with salt and pepper, but gently. Do this for another minute then lower the heat to minimum. In boiled and salted water, boil pasta and once it's cooked al dente turn the heat on your sauté pan with leek and mushroom sauce. Make sure that the water dripping from pasta is also in the pan as you start to toss the pasta and the sauce, add fresh parsley that is finely chopped, drizzle a bit more of olive oil and add just a bit more black pepper. At the end shave some fresh Parmesan and Voila!!

Love at First Taste
Shevid Polo Goosht Loubia

My now ex-husband may say it was love at first sight between the two of us, but I'm pretty sure it was the day he tasted my version of this dish that he realized I was worthy of being his wife. This is the tale of another poor and unappreciated Persian recipe that you won't find in traditional or more modern cookbooks. Shevid Polo Goosht Loubia originates from the great city of Kashan with beautiful, intricately designed Persian carpets hailing from this city as well. This is the Iranians' homage to Osso Bucco, but of course with rice involved.

My ex-husband and his family are big fans of this meal and will keep eating it until the belt buckles come loose and they've licked their plates clean. I cooked it for them one day, knowing that I was still in a place where I was trying to win over my then boyfriend and his family. If you can't impress a man with looks, degrees from Ivy League universities, long legs, pedigree or money, try this recipe and let me know how it goes. For years I've followed the recipe of my beloved and talented cousin, Fay Kashani who's one of the best cooks and bakers I know, and her recipes have never failed to impress me, although I've edited it a bit here.

Unfortunately like food, some marriages have an expiration date too. It's possible this is why I'm so drawn to the kitchen and cooking in general, because we can control our ingredients, we can cut and dice and measure the exact amount we want, but human relationships aren't so predictable. Spring has just come though and I'm excited for new changes, time to cook more food, learn new recipes, and like my grandmother, to put all the love I have left inside of me into all the dishes I've yet to cook. I promise I'll share more with you when the time is right, but for now enjoy these recipes and this moment, which is the greatest feast of all.

The Rice
PREPARATION:

Wash the rice with warm water and add salt and water to it. Let it soak overnight. Wash the dill, let it dry or put it in a salad spinner, then chop finely and put aside (this can be prepared the day before). Bring 8 cups of water to boil in a non stick pot, drain the soaked rice and add to the boiling water, when the rice is al dente or half cooked empty into a strainer. Add oil and butter to the pot. Once the oil has been heated remove from stove top. Add chopped dill in between the rice and back into the pot, and simmer for one hour and fifteen minutes without taking off the lid.

Shevid Polo Goosht Loubia

The Braise

INGREDIENTS:

- **2 lbs veal Shank (some do it with lamb)**
- **1 lb dried white beans**
- **2 large onions**
- **2 tsp turmeric**
- **1½ tsp salt**
- **1 tsp black pepper**
- **1 clove garlic**
- **1 tbsp butter**
- **1 tbsp oil**
- **6-7 cups water (depending on how much it takes for your beans to get soft)**

The Rice:

- **5 bunches of dill**
- **4 cups basmati rice**
- **2 tbsp vegetable oil**
- **2 tbsp butter**
- **1 tbsp salt**

PREPARATION:

Wash the veal shank, wash the dried white beans, peel and cut up the onions in large pieces. Brown the shanks on both sides in a bit of oil and butter and add the onion and garlic to brown a bit. Then add everything to a large Dutch oven, add the turmeric, salt and pepper with 6 cups of water and bring to boil, then simmer at a lower temperature for about 3-4 hours. Serve on top of rice.

Note

Note

...To be continued...